THE
LABRADOR
RETRIEVER

by Charlotte Wilcox

CAPSTONE PRESS
MANKATO, MINNESOTA

C A P S T O N E   P R E S S
818 North Willow Street • Mankato, MN 56001

Printed in the United States of America.

Library of Congress Cataloging-in-Publication Data
Wilcox, Charlotte.
    The Labrador retriever/by Charlotte Wilcox
    p. cm.--(Learning about dogs)
    Includes bibliographical references (p. 46) and index.
    Summary: An introduction to North America's most popular dog, which
    includes its history, development, uses, and care.
    ISBN 1-56065-396-5
    1. Labrador retriever--Juvenile literature. [1. Labrador retriever] I. Title.
    II. Series: Wilcox, Charlotte. Learning about dogs.
SF429.L3W54 1996
636.7'52--dc20

                                                    96-26562
                                                      CIP
3 3187 00124 4843   AC

Photo credits
Sue Reynolds, cover.
Reynolds Photography, 4, 6, 16, 22, 38-39, 40.
Unicorn/Jean Higgins, 8; Jim Shippe, 10; D.F. Bunde, 13, 32;
    John Ebeling, 14; Ted Rose, 18; Jay Foreman, 26;
    Aneal Vohra, 34; Scott Liles, 28, 36.
Bill Smith, 21.
FPG, 24, 30.

Table of Contents

Words in **boldface** type in the text are defined
in the Glossary in the back of this book.

Quick Facts about the Labrador

Description

Height:

Males stand 22-1/2 to 24-1/2 inches (57 to 61 centimeters) and females stand 21-1/2 to 23-1/2 inches (54-1/2 to 59-1/2 centimeters) from the ground to the top of the shoulders.

Weight:

Males weigh 65 to 80 pounds (30 to 36 kilograms) and females weigh 55 to 70 pounds (25 to 32 kilograms).

Physical features: Labs are muscular dogs with short coats, medium-sized ears that fold close to the head, and easily recognized tails that are broad near the body and tapered at the tip.

Color: There are three kinds of Labs, each a different color. They are black, yellow, and chocolate.

Development

Place of origin: Labs originated in Canada.

History of breed: Labs descended from dogs used by fishermen in Labrador in eastern Canada. They were later brought to England as hunting dogs.

Numbers: More than 125,000 Labradors are **registered** every year in the United States. Almost 10,000 are registered in Canada each year. Many more are born but are not registered.

Uses

Labradors make good family pets. They are also used for hunting, law enforcement, and as **guide dogs** for the blind.

Chapter 1
North America's Favorite Dog

The Labrador retriever is the most popular dog in North America. It tops the list of dogs registered with the American and Canadian Kennel Clubs. The Labrador retriever may be the most popular dog in the world. Queen Elizabeth of England owns Labradors. She enters many of her dogs in competitions.

Labrador retrievers are called Labs for short. They are friendly and affectionate. They are reliable dogs that bark but usually do not bite.

Labrador retrievers come in three colors. They are black, chocolate, and yellow.

Labs are handsome. They are calm and obedient. Labs are used for hunting, for showing, and for companionship.

Labradors are suitable for almost any type of job or family. They can live in city apartments or the toughest outdoor conditions. They get along well with other animals, children, and the elderly. Labrador retrievers are eager to please their owners. Maybe that is why they are North America's favorite dog.

Labradors can be trained to help a person with a disability. They can turn on lights and get the mail.

Chapter 2

Beginnings of the Breed

The Labrador retriever is named after the Labrador region in eastern Canada. But **retriever** dogs have not always lived in North America. The Labrador retriever's ancestors came from Europe with fishermen.

Every day for thousands of years, fishing boats pushed off from villages along the shores of Europe. Teams of fishermen worked together, fishing with a huge net. One or two fishermen stood in the water near the shore holding ropes attached to the net.

Labradors were once water dogs that helped fishermen.

When the net was full of fish, everyone
pulled hard on their ropes to close the net. If a
rope broke or the end dropped in the water,
someone would have to swim out to get it. If a
net broke, someone would have to dive
underwater to pick up the broken part. If fish
fell out of the net, someone would have to
retrieve them. The work was hard. The
fishermen were always wet, unless they had a
water dog to help them.

Water Dogs

Water dogs made good helpers for
fishermen. They carried ropes and nets. They
could even pick up fish in their mouths. They
could swim faster than a human wearing heavy
clothes. They could see better underwater.
Fishing was a lot easier and a little drier for a
fisherman who had a water dog.

Fishermen tried to breed dogs that were
good at working in water. The best ones had
coats that shed water easily. They could not
bring a lot of water into the boat. They had to

Labradors are still good at retrieving from water.

be strong enough to carry heavy nets through rough waters. They had to be small enough so a fisherman could lift them into a small boat.

Coming to Newfoundland

Fishermen were among the first Europeans to come to North America almost 500 years ago. They found some of the best fishing in the world near the island of Newfoundland off Canada's eastern coast.

English and Irish fishermen set up a colony on Newfoundland. Among the things they brought with them were their water dogs. It was in North America that these dogs developed into the unique Labrador breed.

The Labrador retriever breed was developed in Newfoundland, Canada.

Chapter 3

Development of the Labrador Retriever

Labrador retrievers have special **traits**. Their tails are different from those of any other breed. The kind expression on a Labrador's face is easy to recognize. Labs are one of the gentlest and most intelligent of all breeds. They come in only three colors. No one knows exactly where these special traits came from.

Two Kinds of Newfoundland Dogs

Fishermen were the only Europeans in Newfoundland for a long time. They made a living selling fish to people back in Europe. They bred two different types of dogs to help them. At first, both of these breeds were called Newfoundland dogs.

One type was a huge dog with a long, thick coat and bushy tail. The large Newfoundland dogs

Labradors love to play. They are gentle and smart.

Labradors can swim well and their coats shed water.

were called Greater Newfoundlands. They worked in the water and also carried packs and pulled carts on land.

Greater Newfoundlands weighed about 150 pounds (68 kilograms). They were large enough to save a man from drowning. But they were too big to fit in small fishing boats.

The smaller Newfoundland dogs were called Lesser Newfoundlands. They were the right size for fishing boats. Their short, oily coats shed water. They could swim well.

When more Europeans arrived, they spread across Newfoundland and onto the Canadian mainland to an area called Labrador. The new arrivals were hunters and farmers. They found that the Lesser Newfoundland dogs did a great job of retrieving **game** birds and animals after they had been shot.

Over to England

News of the intelligent Lesser Newfoundland dogs soon reached England. Canadian fishermen could make just as much money selling their dogs in England as they could selling fish.

During the 1800s, rich Englishmen were trying to breed better hunting dogs. They were always looking for dogs with the traits needed to hunt their favorite kind of game. One breeder, the Earl of Malmesbury, fell in love with a Lesser Newfoundland dog he bought from a Canadian fisherman.

Over the years, the earl bought many Lesser Newfoundlands from Canada. He called his dogs

Labradors so they would not be confused with the larger, long-haired Greater Newfoundlands.

A few other English breeders also bought Labradors for breeding. They kept the breed pure and strong in England.

The Labrador Disappears from Canada

In 1885, the government of Newfoundland passed the Sheep Protection Act. This allowed a heavy license tax on dogs. Since most fishermen and hunters were poor, they could not afford the tax. Many Canadians had to get rid of their dogs. Their best hope was to sell them to good homes in England.

About the same time, the English government passed a **quarantine** law. All animals brought into England had to be quarantined for six months. Canadians who wanted to sell their dogs in England had to pay to feed and care for them in a special kennel for six months. That cost more money than they could get for the dogs.

Canadians were unable to pay the tax and unable to sell their dogs. They simply stopped raising them. Soon there was not one Labrador dog left in Canada. The breed was saved from

Labradors are popular hunting dogs.

extinction in English kennels where some
Labradors already lived. English breeders improved
the breed by crossing Labs with other retrievers.

Making a Comeback

Within a few years, the Labrador retriever
became popular across England as a hunting dog.
With changes in the laws, Labs began making a
comeback in Canada and the United States in the
1930s. Now they are the most popular dog in both
countries.

Chapter 4
The Labrador Retriever Today

Paintings and photographs of Labrador retrievers from the 1800s look much like modern Labs. The Labrador's coat and tail are the most recognized features.

Special Traits

The first thing most people notice in a Labrador retriever is the smooth, glossy coat. The hair is short, straight, and thick. This coat sheds water to keep the Labrador's skin dry when it swims.

Labradors have a kind, gentle expression. Warm, friendly eyes give the Labrador a look all its own. Black and yellow Labs always have brown eyes. Some chocolate Labs have hazel eyes.

Labradors have smooth, glossy coats.

Different colors of Labradors are the same breed.

The tail is a unique feature of a Labrador. It is shaped like an otter's tail. It is round and wide near the body and tapers to a point at the tip. The tail is covered with short, thick hair.

Labradors are medium-sized dogs. Males are 22-1/2 to 24-1/2 inches (57 to 61 centimeters) tall and weigh 65 to 80 pounds (30 to 36 kilograms).

Females are a little smaller. They are 21-1/2 to 23-1/2 inches (54-1/2 to 59-1/2 centimeters) tall and weigh 55 to 70 pounds (25 to 32 kilograms).

Colors

Labrador retrievers are easily recognized by their solid colors. They are black, chocolate, or yellow. They are never spotted or marked except for an occasional small white spot on the chest.

Black Labs are jet black. Chocolates can be light to dark chocolate brown. Yellow Labs can be any shade from light yellow-cream to deep fox-red. Yellows sometimes have lighter or darker shading on the ears, back, and lower parts of the body.

Some people think different colored Labradors are different breeds. This is not true. Labs have all three colors in their **genetic makeup**. A pair of black Labs can have puppies of all three colors. A pair of chocolates can have chocolate or yellow puppies. A pair of yellows can have only yellow puppies.

Chapter 5
The Labrador Retriever in Action

Labrador retrievers do not pull fishnets anymore, but many still work. Labs are used for police work and disaster aid. They also help persons with disabilities. Many Labs still hunt with their owners.

Gun Dogs at Work

Dogs that work with hunters are called **gun dogs**. At a sporting event called a **field trial**, gun dogs and their owners compete in hunting tests. Dogs are judged on how well they find and

Labradors participate in field trials to test their skills.

retrieve birds for the hunter. In North America, Labrador retrievers are top winners at these events.

Labs in Law Enforcement

More and more police units are using Labrador retrievers. One reason is that Labs do not frighten the public like German shepherds and Dobermans sometimes do. Another reason is that Labs have very good noses. The Labrador's strong sense of smell makes it good at finding illegal drugs, bombs, and guns.

Fire departments use Labs to find signs of **arson** in burned buildings. The army sends Labs into areas that might have explosive land mines. Dogs can smell explosives and alert people to where they are without setting them off.

Labradors are especially good for disaster work. Search-and-rescue dogs enter collapsed or burned buildings to look for survivors. They can find trapped people humans would never find. Because Labs are kind and gentle, they are better at lifesaving work than more aggressive breeds.

Because Labs are gentle, they are good working with people.

Helping the Disabled

Many Labrador retrievers are guide dogs for the blind. More than one-third of all guide dogs in North America are Labradors. In England, two-thirds are Labs. In Australia, all guide dogs are Labs.

Blind people like Labradors because they are big enough to take the lead but not too big to handle. Though they are usually obedient, Labradors know to disobey a command if they see danger.

Some Labs are trained as **signal dogs** for deaf people. When the dog hears such important sounds as an alarm clock, smoke alarm, or a crying child, it runs between the sound and its owner until the person notices. If the owner is asleep, the dog nudges the person awake. Other Labs work as **service dogs** for disabled people. They bring in mail, turn lights on and off, and retrieve things.

Many Labradors are guide dogs for the blind.

Chapter 6

A Labrador of Your Own

Labradors make wonderful family pets. That is probably the main reason why they are North America's favorite dog. Some breeds single out one person to love. Labradors love all the members of a family.

Keeping a Lab

Labrador retrievers are easy to keep in the house. They are well behaved when properly trained. They do not shed much hair. Labs need a quiet corner with a food dish, a water

Labradors are North America's favorite dogs.

33

Labradors need to walk or play three times a day.

dish, and a dog bed or cage with a blanket. Labradors like to chew and dig. Shoes and houseplants can be tempting, so provide some chewable toys.

Labradors can take just about any kind of weather except extreme heat. When fully grown, they can be kept outdoors if they have good protection from sun, wind, rain, and snow. You will need a high fence because Labs are good climbers. The fence should be buried one foot (30 centimeters) in the ground because Labs are good at digging, too.

Labradors need to walk or play at least three times a day. Labs love to swim, play catch, and explore.

To make sure you find your dog if it gets lost, have your name and telephone number engraved on the collar. Or have a **veterinarian** implant a microchip under its skin. A microchip is a computer chip about the size of a grain of rice. When scanned, it will tell the owner's name, address, and telephone number.

Feeding a Labrador

The best diet for a Labrador retriever is dry dog food. A full-grown Lab may eat a pound (half a kilogram) or more of food a day. One

**Labradors are comfortable when they have a space that
is all their own.**

meal a day is fine, or you can divide it in two.
Labradors can put on weight if they are fed
more than they need.

Dogs need plenty of water. Have fresh water
out all the time, or make sure your dog drinks
at least three times a day.

Grooming

Labradors do not need much grooming. A gentle brushing once a day or so is usually enough. If the dog gets dirty or muddy, wash the dirt off with clear water. Give a bath with soap only when absolutely necessary. Even gentle dog shampoo removes oil from the coat and dries out the skin.

Give your dog a rawhide bone to chew to help keep its teeth healthy. Chewing on a carrot or apple is also good. Clean your dog's teeth with a soft, wet brush or cloth. Trim your dog's nails if they get too long. Ask your veterinarian to show you how it is done.

Health Care

Dogs need shots every year to protect them from serious diseases that can kill them and spread to humans. They need pills to protect them from **heartworms**. Dogs should have a checkup every year for all types of worms.

During warm weather, check for ticks. Some ticks carry **Lyme disease** that can cripple an

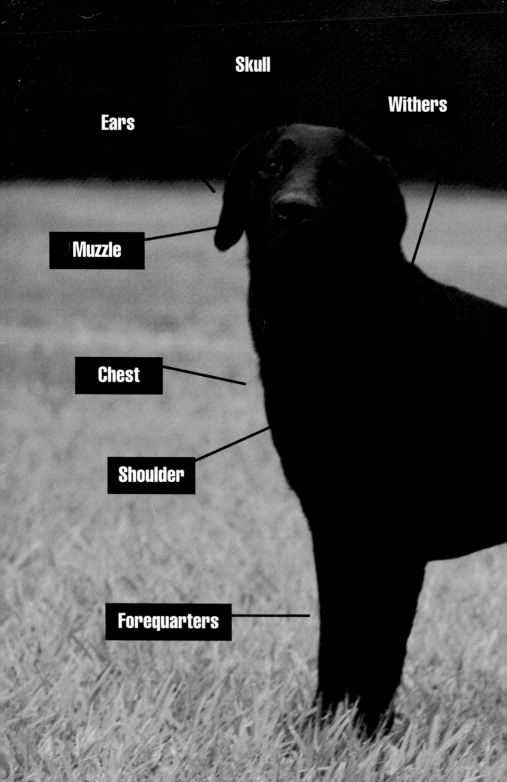

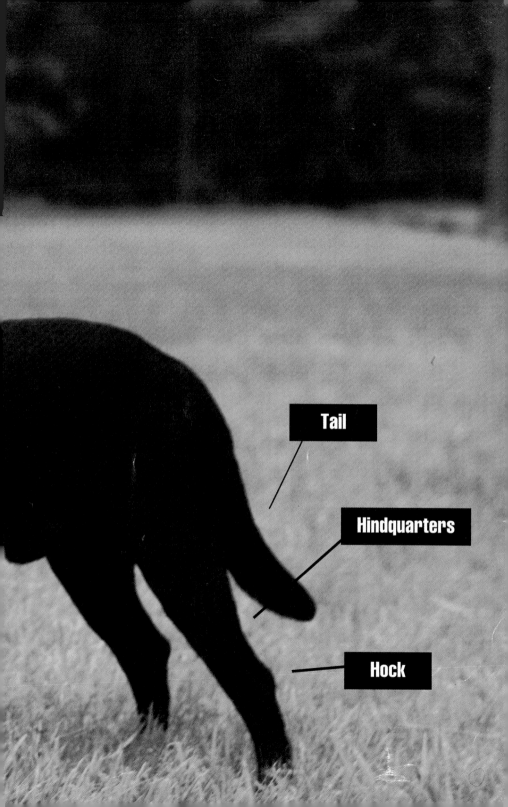

Tail

Hindquarters

Hock

A Labrador retriever club can help you find a puppy.

animal or human. Put rubbing alcohol on the tick and pull it out with tweezers. Drown the tick in the alcohol or bleach. Check often for fleas, lice, and mites.

Looking for a Labrador

If you are looking for a puppy, contact the Labrador retriever club in your area to find a good breeder. You may also be able to get a Labrador at a rescue shelter. Check with your local Labrador retriever club for shelters in your area.

Rescue shelters find homes for dogs that are orphaned for one reason or another. Shelters usually charge a small fee to cover expenses. Some shelters offer the dogs free. Many of the dogs are trained and have been checked for health problems.

When you find a Labrador of your own, you will know why it is North America's favorite dog.

Quick Facts about Dogs

Dog Terms

A male is simply called a dog. A female dog is called a bitch. A young dog is a puppy until it is one year old. A newborn puppy is a whelp until it is **weaned**. A family of puppies born at one time is called a litter.

Life History

Origin: All dogs, wolves, coyotes, and **dingoes** descended from a single wolflike dog. Dogs have been friends of humans since earliest times.

Types: There are many colors, shapes, and sizes of dogs. Full-grown dogs weigh from two pounds (one kilogram) to more than 200 pounds (90 kilograms). They are from six inches (15 centimeters) to three feet (90 centimeters) tall. They can have thick hair or almost no hair, long or short legs, and many types of ears, faces, and tails. There are about 350 different dog breeds in the world.

Reproductive life: Dogs mature at six to 18 months. Puppies are born two months after breeding. A female can have two litters per year. An average litter is three to six puppies, but litters of 15 or more are possible.

Development: Puppies are born blind and deaf. Their ears and eyes open at one to two weeks. They try to walk at about two weeks. At three weeks, their teeth begin to come in, and they are ready to start weaning.

Life span:	Dogs are fully grown at two years. If well cared for, they may live about 15 years.

The Dog's Super Senses

Smell:	Dogs have a sense of smell many times stronger than a human's. Dogs use their supersensitive noses even more than their eyes and ears. They recognize people, animals, and objects just by smelling them, sometimes from long distances away or for days afterward.
Hearing:	Dogs hear far better than humans. Not only can dogs hear things from farther away, they can hear high-pitched sounds people cannot.
Sight:	Dogs are **color-blind**. Some scientists think dogs can tell some colors. Others think dogs see everything in black and white. Dogs can see twice as wide around them as humans can because their eyes are on the sides of their heads.
Touch:	Dogs enjoy being petted more than almost any other animal. They can feel vibrations like an approaching train or an earthquake soon to happen.
Taste:	Dogs do not taste much. This is partly because their sense of smell is so strong that it overpowers the taste. It is also partly because they swallow their food too quickly to taste it well.
Navigation:	Dogs can often find their way through crowded streets or across miles of wilderness without any guidance. This is a special dog sense that scientists do not fully understand.

Glossary

arson—the crime of intentionally setting property on fire

color-blind—unable to see colors or the difference between colors

dingo—wild Australian dog

field trial—an event where hunting dogs are judged on their ability to find and retrieve game

game—hunted wild animals and birds

genetic makeup—a map of genes that determines characteristics

guide dog—a dog trained to lead a blind person

gun dog—a dog trained to find and retrieve game that has been shot

heartworm—tiny worm carried by mosquitoes that enters a dog's heart and slowly destroys it

Lyme disease—a disease carried by ticks that causes illness, pain, and sometimes paralysis in animals and humans

quarantine—keeping people or animals by themselves, either to see if they have a disease or to keep a known disease from spreading

register—to record a dog's breeding records with a kennel club

retriever—a type of dog bred and trained to retrieve dead or wounded game

service dog—a dog trained to help a disabled person

signal dog—a dog trained to help people who cannot hear

trait—a characteristic passed on from parents to offspring

veterinarian—a person trained and qualified to treat the diseases and injuries of animals

wean—to stop nursing or depending on a mother's milk

To Learn More

Alderton, David. *Dogs*. New York: Dorling Kindersley, 1993.

American Kennel Club. *The Complete Dog Book*. New York: Macmillan Publishing, 1992.

Curtis, Patricia. *Greff, the Story of a Guide Dog*. New York: Lodestar Books, 1982.

Jessel, Camilla. *The Puppy Book*. Cambridge, Mass.: Candlewick Press, 1992.

Ring, Elizabeth. *Assistance Dogs: In Special Service*. Brookfield, Conn.: The Millbrook Press, 1993.

Rosen, Michael J. *Kids' Best Field Guide to Neighborhood Dogs*. New York: Workman, 1993.

You can read articles about Labrador retrievers in *AKC Gazette*, *Dog Fancy*, *Dog World*, and *Gun Dog* magazines.

Useful Addresses and Internet Sites

American Kennel Club
5580 Centerview Drive
Raleigh, NC 27606
E-mail address: info@akc.org
http://www.akc.org/akc/

Canadian Kennel Club
100–89 Skyway Avenue
Etobicoke, ON M9W 6R4
Canada

Labrador Retriever Club
P.O. Box 454
Chesterland, OH 44026
E-mail address: 76276.331@compuserve.com

Dog Owner's Guide
http://www.canismajor.com/dog/
Labrador Retriever Home Page
http://www-leland.stanford.edu/~lizalee/labbers
Working Retriever Central
http://starsouth.com/wrc

Index